Hair Loss

How to Stop Hair Loss

Actionable Steps to Stop Hair Loss

(Hair Loss Cure, Hair Care, Natural Hair Loss Cures)

PS: I Owe You!

Thank you for stopping by.

My name is Antony and I am passionate about teaching people literally everything I know about different aspects of life. I am an author and a ghostwriter. I run a small ghostwriting company with slightly over 100 writers. My wife (Faith) and I manage the business along with several other members of the team (editors).

Nice to meet you!

I started publishing (at Fantonpublishers.com) because I'd love to impart the knowledge I gather every single day in my line of work (reading and editing over 10 ghostwritten books every single day). My ghostwriting company deals with literally every topic under the sun, which puts me at a very unique position to learn more in a month than I learnt in my 4 years as a Bachelor of Commerce, Accounting, student. I am constantly answering questions from my friends, relatives and even strangers on various topics that I come across every day at work.

After several years of helping people to achieve different goals (e.g. weight loss, making money online, human resources, management, investing, stress reduction, depression, budgeting, saving etc.) offline thanks to my 'street' as well as 'class' knowledge on different topics, I realized I could be of better help to the world by publishing what I learn. My books are a reflection of what I have been gathering over the years. That's why they are not just focused on one niche but every niche possible out there.

If you would love to be part of my lovely audience who want to change multiple aspects of their life, subscribe to our newsletter http://bit.ly/2fantonpubnewbooks or follow us on social media to receive notifications whenever we publish new books on any niche. You can also send me an email; I would love to hear from you!

PS: Valuable content is my bread and butter. And since I have lots of it to go around, I can share it freely (not everything is about money - changing lives comes first!)

I promise; I am busy just as you are and won't spam (I hate spam too)!

Antony,

Website: http://www.fantonpublishers.com/

Email: Support@fantonpublishers.com

Twitter: https://twitter.com/FantonPublisher

Facebook Page: https://www.facebook.com/Fantonpublisher/

Private Facebook Group For Readers:
https://www.facebook.com/groups/FantonPublishers/

Pinterest: https://www.pinterest.com/fantonpublisher/

Some of the best things in life are free, right?

As a sign of good faith, I will start by giving out content that will help you to implement not only everything I teach in this book but in every other book I write. The content is about life transformation, presented in bit size pieces for easy implementation. I believe that without such a checklist, you are likely to have a hard time implementing anything in this book and any other thing you set out to do religiously and sticking to it for the long haul. It doesn't matter whether your goals relate to weight loss, relationships, personal finance, investing, personal development, improving communication in your family, your overall health, finances, improving your sex life, resolving issues in your relationship, fighting PMS successfully, investing, running a successful business, traveling etc. With a checklist like the one I will show you, you can bet that anything you do will seem a lot easier to implement until the end. This checklist will help you to start well and not lose steam along the way, until the very end. Therefore, even if you don't continue reading this book, at least read the one thing that will help you in every other aspect of your life.

Send me a message on support@fantonpublishers.com and I will send you my 5 Pillar Life Transformation Checklist.

Your life will never be the same again (if you implement what's in this book), I promise.

Introduction

According to statistics, about 35 million men and 21 million women suffer from hair loss with the problem kicking in mostly from the age of 40 years, although many people still experience hair loss much earlier!

Don't let hair loss damage your self-esteem when you can do something to reverse the situation!

Losing hair can be psychologically challenging for many people, especially if that happens when you are still young. Well, let's be honest, none of us wants to have a bald head irrespective of how old we are. However, it is somewhat comforting to lose hair when a good percentage of your age mates are experiencing the same problem. You don't feel as if there is something wrong with you; it feels normal.

If your hair loss does not feel normal and you want to keep your youthful demeanor for a few more years, then you want to make sure that hair loss does not become a menace. You do that by taking action at the earliest sign of receding hair.

My search to deal with thinning hair and hair loss enabled me to come across several concoctions as well as fallacies about hair loss and cures for this problem. In my research, I found out that there is no one particular cure that treats the problem but rather, you would need to embrace several strategies and tactics to cure your hair loss problem.

This book evaluates the various things you can do to cure your hair loss problem.

More precisely, this book focuses on:

- Busting myths that surround hair loss
- **The causes of hair loss**
- How to use herbs and supplement to stop, reverse and prevent hair loss
- **How to use different topical treatments to stop, reverse and prevent hair loss**
- How to make different lifestyle changes to stop, reverse and prevent hair loss
- **How to use different oils to stop, reverse and prevent hair loss**
- When to seek medical help to stop, reverse and prevent hair loss
- **And much, much more!**

If you are uncomfortable about that receding hairline, this book has all you need to make your problems go away. All you need to do is to read it then take action!

I hope you enjoy it!

Table of Contents

PS: I Owe You!... 2

Introduction 6

What Causes Hair Loss?...12

   Myths About Hair Loss 12

   Causes Of Hair Loss 15

Herbs And Supplements 18

Eat To Achieve Fast Hair Growth................................. 24

Foods That Cause Hair Loss... 35

Topical Treatments 38

Lifestyle Changes... 65

Preventive Oils 67

   How To Use Preventive Oils For Hair Care............... 70

Ways of Caring for Your Hair Naturally 71

Medical Assistance 74

Conclusion.. 75

Do You Like My Book & Approach To Publishing?...... 76

6 Things.. 76

1: First, I'd Love It If You Leave a Review of This Book on Amazon. 77

2: Check Out My Other Books 77

3: Let's Get In Touch 78

4: Grab Some Freebies On Your Way Out; Giving Is Receiving, Right? 79

5: Suggest Topics That You'd Love Me To Cover To Increase Your Knowledge Bank. 79

6: Subscribe To My Newsletter To Know When I Publish New Books. 79

My Other Books 81

Weight Loss Books 81

General Weight Loss Books 81

Weight Loss Books On Specific Diets 82

Ketogenic Diet Books 82

Intermittent Fasting Books 82

Any Other Diet 82

Relationships Books 83

Personal Development 83

Personal Finance & Investing Books 84

Health & Fitness Books 84

Book Summaries 85
All The Other Niches 85
See You On The Other Side! 87
Stay With Me On My Journey To Making Passive Income Online 88
PSS: Let Me Also Help You Save Some Money! 90

© **Copyright 2018 by Fantonpublishers.com - All rights reserved**.

What Causes Hair Loss?

Everyone loses 50 to a hundred strands of hair each day, which is absolutely normal. Thus, if you are losing more than these numbers of strands, then there could be a big problem. The hair loss could simply be a sign of other serious medical conditions that you may not even realize. Thus, it is usually important to see the doctor immediately you notice that you are losing handfuls of hair. The treatment for hair loss is usually different since the causes of hair loss are also diverse. Thus, we will evaluate the different myths surrounding hair loss and actual causes of hair loss in order to be in a position to address your hair loss solution more comprehensively.

Myths About Hair Loss

There are several myths surrounding hair loss that you need to know about to avoid being deceived. These myths include:

Diets can cause hair loss

A balanced diet is suitable for general health. However, no proven statistics have shown that certain types of food cause hair loss.

Hair loss comes from your mother's side

This is not entirely true since even though the gene for baldness is associated with the x chromosome, other factors also play a critical part in hair loss. Research indicates that if a man has a father who is bald, he is likely to become bald too.

Wearing hats strains the hair follicles, which make the hair to fall out

If you wear a hat frequently, you do not have to worry about causing your hair to fall out. What you need to ensure is to have a clean hat as a dirty one can lead to an infection of the scalp, which can accelerate hair loss.

If you are balding, you are old

On the contrary, teens and people in their twenties and thirties can experience balding. However, the earlier it begins, the more severe it will be.

Exposure to the sun causes balding

Too much exposure of the sun can cause other skin conditions but not balding. Tanning beds also cannot make one bald.

Sexually active men become bald first

This is completely not true since research has show that bald headed men do not have more testosterone than those who are not bald.

Losing hair each day means that you are balding

Well, you will lose hair each day if you have male-pattern baldness. However, it is normal to lose as many as 100 hairs each day, since they normally grow back.

Excessive washing of hair is likely to cause hair loss

Washing hair frequently does not on itself cause hair loss but rather too much manipulation done when the hair is wet. As we all know, hair is weak when wet; thus, if you are always washing your hair, you have to detangle frequently leading to little hair loss. This hair however grows back quickly.

Wigs and weaves cause hair loss

Most people say that hair needs to breathe and if it does not, this can lead to hair loss. This is a lie since the hair needs not to breathe since roots are the only ones that are alive, and they get oxygen from blood within the scalp. Hairpieces like wigs will only cause damage if they are extremely tight.

Causes Of Hair Loss

What can make you lose your hair more than normal varies. This makes it critical to analyze the different causes of hair loss in order to know the appropriate solutions for different causes of hair loss.

Hereditary hair loss

Androgenetic alopecia, is hair loss that is genetic and is one of the common causes of hair loss. This gene can be inherited from either the father's or the mother's side. However, it is likely to be more pronounced if both of your parents have it. In women, the hairline may start thinning behind the bangs and may even spread to the entire scalp. In order to know whether the cause of hair loss is genetic, the dermatologist usually observes the pattern of hair loss. Further tests may be a biopsy of your scalp, which may be done to see if hair follicles have been replaced with miniaturized follicles. When suffering from hereditary hair loss, you may not necessarily cure hair loss since it is in your genetic makeup; however, you can slow down the process.

Medical conditions

Suffering from certain medical conditions increases your likelihood of suffering from hair loss. For instance, if you have thyroid problems, you may have suffer hair loss since the thyroid gland regulates your hormone levels; thus, if it is not working properly you may lose some hair. Scalp infections like ringworm can also lead to hair loss. Other skin conditions like some types of lupus can lead to permanent hair loss. Suffering from Alopecia areata will also lead to hair loss since when you have this condition; the hair follicles are attacked by the immune system leading to small roundish patches of hair loss. Furthermore, drugs for treating medical conditions like high blood pressure, cancer, arthritis and depression are also known to cause hair loss. Thus, you should be careful if you are taking any drugs for treating these conditions.

Polycystic ovarian syndrome is also a common cause of hair loss. Over five million women in the United States suffer from this condition. The condition can begin as early as the age of 11. It is usually caused by a hormonal imbalance where the ovaries produce too many male hormones. Suffering from PCOS can easily cause fertility. One of the common symptoms of this condition is that you start to experience facial hair growth, and irregular periods. You may then lose hair on your scalp although have hair growing on other parts of the body

Hair pulling disorder

This is normally a sort of mental illness that makes people have an irresistible urge to pull our their hair. This could be puling hair from the eyebrows, scalp and even other parts of the body. The continued pulling of hair can lead to bald spots on the head.

Emotional or physical Shock

Several people may also experience thinning of hair for a certain period after an emotional or physical shock. Thus, if anything drastic happens in your life, and you start experiencing thinning of hair, you do not have to be alarmed, as this phase will pass. However, it is critical to find ways of managing the hair loss.

Certain hairstyles

Quite a number of women are guilty of having hairstyles that pull their hairs too tightly. Thus, having cornrows, pigtail and buns can lead to traction hair loss. Always make sure that you hair is not pulled too tight when putting a weave or getting cornrows. While these styles may look good, it can be disastrous if you experience hair loss because of certain behaviors.

What to expect during and after hair loss

Hair loss normally has a number of effects. It is usually associated with psychological and emotional effects. You are likely to experience stress if your hair is lost leaving your scalp bald. Hair loss may also lead to genetic and underactive thyroid and other health conditions.

Due to the effects normally associated with hair loss, it is important for you to understand the different solutions you can use to address your hair loss problem.

Herbs And Supplements

There are a number of herbs that are known to treat hair loss or reduce the rate at which you may be losing your hair. I will thus look at these herbs and supplements, as well as the most suitable way to use them to enjoy maximum benefits from their use.

Use of saw palmetto

Saw palmetto is used to generally promote healthy hair and skin. It is also important as it blocks the production of a metabolite of testosterone that is actually a contributing factor to the enlarging of the prostate. This metabolite of testosterone as well has a negative direct effect on hair as it usually causes hair loss. Since the saw palmetto is known to hinder the production of this metabolite of testosterone, it can come in handy in slowing or stopping hair loss. In most cases, the product has been proved very effective especially in men. It also works well in women though not effectively, as it does for men.

Hair Supplements

Sometimes, the human body does not get enough nutrients to support hair development hence necessitating supplementation.

Hair supplements are important in stopping breakage or shedding of hair, promoting growth of long and thicker hair as well as ensuring a healthy scalp.

The ability of hair supplements to somewhat offer a conditioning property will lead to smooth and lustrous hair free from toxins and other damaging elements. The effects of nicely moisturized hair starting from the root up to the hair shaft can easily revive and improve your hair's natural sheen. Hair supplements also help improve the generation of sebum, an oily substance that makes hair lustrous.

Especially when natural or organically made, hair supplements come in various products with different ingredients to ensure healthy hair. There are many benefits of using hair products which depends on the active ingredients included in the package.

1: Increased Hair Elasticity

By buying hair supplements, you will enjoy increased hair elasticity and protection from occasional drying or hair breakage. Most hair supplements contain ingredients such as vitamin A and biotin, a B-complex vitamin that is effective in producing keratin. Hair supplements that contain Vitamin C are also effective in stopping hair loss, fighting dandruff as well as inhibiting the loss of hair.

2: Stimulated hair Growth

Hair supplements also stimulate hair growth especially in cases of hair loss or balding. Many hair products contain antioxidants that can improve the immune system while increasing blood and nutrients supply to different parts of the body including the scalp. The supply of important substances to the scalp ensures that growth of hair is stimulated, and you can start experiencing hair growth almost immediately. Products that contain vitamin E and other antioxidants are necessary in improving blood circulation in the hair follicles, which enhances hair growth.

3: Prevention from graying

Hair supplements that contain biotin and vitamin E also offer you added benefits such as prevention from graying of the hair, a condition that may be as a result of aging. The graying of hair is a persistent problem that is mostly caused by oxidation of hair tissues.

The antioxidants present in various hair supplements ensure that corrosion between tissues is minimized, preventing premature graying. If already experiencing hair loss and other dermatological issues, you should try a number of hair products specifically made to address your individual problem.

4: Improved Hair quality and Texture

Hair supplements can also improve the hair quality and texture while at the same time cleansing the dead cells from hair follicles and other accumulated dead layers. Naturally, human follicles may die temporarily, followed by occasional rebirth of new cells that will favor growth of new hair on the skin.

Some conditions such as baldness and trauma may make the follicles to die permanently, a situation that can be prevented by supplementing with hair products. The products are also important as they contain antioxidants that assist in neutralizing free radicals in hair scalp.

5: Repairing Split Ends

Hair supplements are very vital in repairing split ends and other hair damages that may result from curling, blow drying or dyeing of the hair. These hair problems are treatable with hair products containing vitamin E, a compulsory ingredient that is a must-have for all supplements.

Opting for hair growth supplements is one of the most effective methods to treat hair loss. But when purchasing an effective and natural type of a hair supplement, few considerations are important to observe. This is due to the many varieties of different hair products available in the markets with each promising to be best.

So the key here is to know what you want! But what does this really mean especially if you're trying them for your very first time?

Obviously, no two supplements have identical purposes. Some supplements will be ideal for making your hair stronger while others will help in dealing with dandruff and perhaps others will help in restoring natural hair growth. You need to be very specific on what you want to achieve. Do you want to grow your hair? Do you want to prevent hair loss? Or do you want to make your hair stronger. Answering these questions could provide the key to choosing the most suitable supplements.

On top of buying hair growth supplements, eating foods rich in vitamins is a sure way to naturally reverse hair loss or baldness.

Vitamins

Consumption of foods that are generally rich in vitamins can contribute greatly to curbing the problem of hair loss. A number of people only have the idea that the vitamins are good for their health but they do not know whether the vitamins they take play great role in their hair.

For this reason, you need to add more milligrams of vitamins in your meal to ensure that you provide vitamins for your body cells and you hair.

For instance, vitamin A is an anti-oxidant for your hair and it functions to promote healthy production of sebum in the scalp. Sebum is normally an oily substance that is made of lipids and debris of dead fat-producing cells. Sebum mainly functions to protect and waterproof hair and skin. It actually keeps the hair from becoming dry, brittle or cracked as this can cause hair loss. Moreover, sebum functions to inhibit the growth of microorganisms on the skin as they may as well have negative effects to the skin and the hair.

Food that is rich in vitamin E is also vital, as vitamin E is very important as it stimulates blood circulation. You need to note that proper blood circulation in the scalp is vital as it helps in keeping the hair follicles productive ensuring less damage of cells and this eventually prevents hair loss.

All B vitamins are as well important in maintenance of your hair. This is because vitamin B helps your body to produce melanin a substance that actually gives the hair its black color. Melanin as well provides natural protection against the harmful effects of UV rays of the sun to the skin and the hair as they usually cause damage of cells around the skin including hair follicles thus causing hair loss.

Hair Loss

Talking about vitamins, did you know that you can use diet to both fight hair loss and promote natural growth of thick and healthy hair? Whether you are seeking to recover from a misguided haircut or maybe wishing to grow a natural long hair, you can achieve your desired look with patience and good diet. Investing your time on good diet is a strategy recommended by most hair stylists and yield good results.

Here is a list of foods you should consider eating together with the benefits or properties they possess.

Eat To Achieve Fast Hair Growth

The rule of the thumb is to eat more high-protein foods!

Consumption of foods that are normally rich in proteins can as well help in curbing the problem of hair loss. Eating lean meat, eggs and other suitable sources of proteins is quite advisable. This is because hair and nails are mostly made up of proteins thus in case of protein deficiency in the body, all the bode cells especially the hair cells will be greatly affected and for hair, the most likely effect for this is increased rate of hair loss leading to baldness and other emotional and psychological effects resulting from hair loss.

For instance, protein is also an important building block of blood thus it deficiency in the body would mean that the blood capacity would be reduced leading to improper blood circulation. Blood deficiency especially to the scalp would lead to increased hair loss. Therefore, to avoid such situations, you need to incorporate many foods with high portions of protein in your food, as you would as well ensure healthy growth of your hair.

Here are the most recommended protein-rich foods you should consider along with related hair growth promoting foods:

Fatty Fish

Fish such as salmon is rich in proteins and vitamin D which are important for enhancing strong and healthy hair. Majority of cold water fish such as salmon contain omega-3 fatty acids, needed by your body to facilitate fast hair growth. These fatty acids are present on the cell membranes, and are often replenished by the natural oil produced by your scalp.

Research shows that you need omega-3 fatty acids to reduce instances of hair loss and to boost hair density. Related studies also reveal that supplementing with fish oil can greatly help prevent hair loss and boost hair growth in women with thin hair.

Apart from salmon, shrimp is among sea foods rich in zinc, a nutrient that promotes hair growth by blocking possible loss of hair. Shrimp contains zinc in the form that it attaches to your glands that connects to hair follicles. Eating more shrimp prevent your hair from thinning. The recommended amount of zinc per day is around 11 milligrams. You can also eat mackerel and herring for an extra boost of omega-3 fatty acids for increased hair growth and hair density.

Oysters

If you aren't a fan of salmon or shrimp, try oysters for fast and healthy growth of hair. They are rich in zinc, a mineral whose deficiency leads to a flaky scalp, dry scalp and loss of hair. Zinc is required in the synthesis of androgens, which affects growth of hair.

Lack of androgen or rather zinc deficiency is attributed to slow hair growth together with stubborn and reoccurring dandruff. Research has shown that dietary zinc can effectively reverse hair loss compared to taking zinc supplements which normally have higher doses of the mineral to the extent of causing hair loss.

To reverse hair loss and to boost the rate of hair growth, try consuming oysters or a mackerel for good results. An Indian mackerel is also rich in omega 3 and omega 6, which helps to rejuvenate your scalp and encourage efficient growth of follicles.

Healthy hair follicles instead assist in accelerated growth of thick and healthy hair.

Lean Meat

Research has shown that to some extent, loss of hair and baldness can be caused by lack or inadequate amounts of iron in the diet. In most cases, women tend to be iron deficient resulting into thin and unhealthy hair growth. Consuming red meat is an effective method of boosting the iron intake and thus fast and healthy growth of hair. Beef is one of the healthiest and effective lean meats for hair growth that reduces hair loss and also boosts the rate of hair growth. This is because red meat has iron mineral that is easier to absorb and this facilitates transport of oxygen throughout the hair follicles.

A good complement to lean meat is the liver which contains the highest amount of biotin, which is a form of B complex vitamin that aids in fast hair and nail growth. Though you may find liver not to be as appetizing as should be, it's a healthy food choice when it comes to your hair. Find a good way of preparing the liver to obtain the highest amount of biotin you can ever wish for.

Eggs

They are good for your hair thanks to their 4 vital properties among them iron, sulfur, selenium and zinc. Eggs are also rich in biotin, a kind of vitamin B that facilitates fast growth of hair.

Apart from these nutrients, eggs are rich in proteins, which assist in oxygen supply to the hair follicles. The omega-3 fatty acid in eggs is important in hair growth together with Vitamin B5 and B12 that triggers growth of hair.

The healthiest part of the egg is the egg yolk as egg whites might block the uptake of biotin into your body, thus resulting into its depletion. To avoid loss of hair and other related issues, eat ample of egg yolks to boost the supply of biotin, iron and proteins for fast and healthy growth of hair. Egg yolks also boost the supply of oxygen to the hair follicles to promote hair growth.

Low-Fat Dairy Products

Yoghurt and skim milk are great calcium sources, a mineral that triggers hair growth. These dairy products also contain casein, a high quality source of protein for your hair.

Get these benefits by mixing yoghurt or skim milk with a few tablespoons of ground walnuts or flaxseeds to obtain both zinc and omega-3 fatty acids. Cottage cheese is another dairy product that supplies calcium, whey proteins, casein and proteins. The easiest way is to use cottage cheese in your gravy in case you don't like its bland taste.

Alternatively, try out Greek Yoghurt which contains vitamins B and D, proteins and Calcium, along with an important ingredient referred to as *Pantothenic acid*. This acid comes from vitamin B5 that is found in Greek yoghurt and is always included in most hair products.

Pantothenic acid is required for growth of hair follicles thus allowing fast hair growth.

Lentils and Beans

Lentils are rich in biotin, iron, proteins, and zinc; minerals that help supplement the follicles and in development of healthy hair scalp. Lentils are form of tiny edible pulse that is grown for its lens-shaped seed as a basic food.

Lentil family is made up of kidney beans, black eyed peas, soy beans and channay. Despite their tiny size, they are also rich in folic acid, a property, which allows oxygen to reach the scalp and skin, thus boost hair growth and renewal of cells.

You can enjoy benefits of lentils by tossing them into soup or salad or into other basic food to facilitate fast growth. Lentils are healthy and recommended food for meat eaters, vegans and vegetarians. Furthermore, legumes such as soy beans and kidney beans are important in offering hair support and its maintenance. Garbanzo beans also known as chick peas are rich sources of zinc, vitamin B6 and proteins; which all work together to reduce hair loss and encourage growth. 100 grams of black beans offers 10 percent of your daily zinc requirement.

Dark Green Leafy Vegetables

Dark Green Leafy Vegetables like broccoli are rich in essential vitamins and minerals such as Vitamin A, C, zinc, folic acid and other nutrients required to promote healthy and fast hair growth.

Broccoli has additional minerals such as calcium and folic acid to protect you from baldness and to boost growth of thick and healthy hair. Broccoli is also loaded with vitamins A and C and help in generating sebum, the oil found in the scalp that helps in conditioning the hair naturally.

Likewise kale is considered a super food in that it offers multiple benefits ranging from weight loss to strong healthy hair. It's rich in iron that allows the hair to grow fast and healthy. Lack of iron is documented to cause loss of hair at the temples, a condition that even stretches further than ordinary balding caused by aging.

In addition, try out spinach that has excellent amounts of vitamin A and C, beta carotene, folate and iron which keep your scalp healthy to facilitate smooth circulation of oils into the scalp. Folate is needed in production of red blood cells, while iron is responsible for distribution of oxygen into the cells. Lack of iron causes anemia, which in turn causes stunted hair growth and hair loss. Spinach is a super-food that your body needs to keep your hair follicles moisturized, and also functions as the natural conditioner for your hair.

Non-Leafy Veggies

Vegetables such as sweet potatoes are known for their ability to facilitate thick hair growth within a short period. Sweet potatoes have sufficient amounts of anti-oxidant called beta carotene that is processed into vitamin A in your body.

This vitamin is important in boosting the production of sebum, whose main role is to keep your hair healthy. Vitamin A also helps fasten the rate of hair growth, facilitate growth of thicker hair and also hinder regression of hair follicles. You should eat sufficient amount of sweet potatoes to maintain production of sebum at required levels for healthy scalp.

You should also eat tomatoes as these stop loss or damage of hair, since they are rich in an antioxidant known as lycopene. This antioxidant facilitates growth of hair and prevents balding.

Another veggie to adopt is yellow peppers, which despite their sour taste, eating of pepper greatly boost growth of hair. Peppers are rich in vitamin C whose deficiency results into weak hair, dull and dry hair that may even fall off. Vitamin C is required in synthesis of collagen, a type of fiber that is required to produce new hair cells. Lack of vitamin C can inhibit absorption of vitamin C, making it important for you to consider eating peppers together with iron-rich diet.

Also add in beets and artichokes as these are rich in B vitamins, an essential mineral in majority of supplements claiming to boost the rate of hair growth. B vitamins include riboflavin and biotins and have been scientifically proven to promote fast and healthy hair growth. Lack of B vitamins into your diet can result into loss of hair or thin hair.

Fruits

Fruits range from oranges, kiwis, berries, straw berries and gooseberries, which have rich content of vitamin C that is important for healthy hair.

Deficiency of the vitamin is attributed to hair loss or breakage and thus you need fruits to grow healthy hair. The most recommended fruits are berries, which are rich in iron that reduces the loss of hair and also help the body absorb the mineral into the blood. Berries are also rich in vitamin C that help the body absorb iron which boasting of having lesser calories.

Another fruit to reach for is avocado that is known for it rich amounts of fatty acids, which facilitate smooth and soft scalp. When consumed or directly applied to hair, it triggers the collagen and the elastin, two products which cause the scalp and hair to soften. Furthermore, a medium avocado offer 21 percent of your daily vitamin E requirement, a vitamin that research shows can boost hair growth within a period of 8 months. To get good results, incorporate sour cream as a way to wash the hair to compliment the effect of eating avocados. Sour cream contains lactic acid, which is effective for clearing residual on the scalp while still exfoliating the dead skin. Avocados can greatly boost growth of new hair and also lengthens the existing hair.

Olive oil

This is a perfect choice if seeking for long, shiny and soft hair. Most people do not prefer dry and luster-less hair brought about by following a diet that is too low in fats. Fats are needed for their role in helping the body absorb vitamins required for growth of hair. Fats allow assimilation of vitamin A, D, E, and K into the blood stream.

This oil is effective in growing hair and restoring the shine into your hair. Olive oil also contains anti-oxidants and vitamins and can help seal in moisture in the hair. You can use olive oil to cook food and also apply directly on the hair. The most recommended way of applying olive oil is using it directly on the hair but avoid touching your skin. Let the oil rest overnight with a shower cap and rinse with soap the following morning.

Soy

This is a good choice for hair growth due to the amount of proteins found in soy and soy products. Your hair is made of a protein that is known as keratin, a protein composed of amino acids.

Eating sufficient amino acids that come from soy can make your hair grow faster and be healthy and thick. The hair needs amino acids to boost hair growth and to get additional proteins it requires to grow.

Soy also has high amounts of *spermidine* a compound that research has found out that it triggers growth of long and thicker hair. In fact, spermidine-based nutritional program helps prolong *anagen phase*, or the active hair growth phase characterized with growth of longer hair.

Soy is also rich in iron, a component that helps in the transportation of oxygen into the body and into the hair follicles. Iron also allows your body to utilize the protein obtained from soy and other foods such as eggs, lean meat and beans. Tofu is a soy based food that has sufficient amounts of iron, which minimizes loss of hair. Just a cup serving of tofu has 6.7 mg of iron. You need about 18mg of iron daily.

Nuts and Seeds

Top on the list of nuts are walnuts and almonds, which are the healthiest hair foods you can ever get as they have a lot of vitamin E, biotin and Omega 3.

Hair Loss

A cup of almonds has almost a 1/3 of your daily requirement of biotin, thus taking almonds can grow your hair to considerable length within few weeks. On the other hand, 28 grams of almonds (1 ounce) offers you 37 percent of vitamin E required in a day.

For walnut, its rich in Omega-3 fatty acid as well as copper, that maintains healthy and brightly colored hair. Actually, they have all you need for faster hair growth among them the building blocks that result to fast and high quality hair. They include proteins, which constitute the building blocks of hair, vitamin E and biotin, which triggers faster hair growth. You should take about ½ cup of walnuts to start witnessing accelerated hair growth to your amazement.

For seeds, top on the list is sunflower seeds, which just a little amount of these seeds can offer sufficient amounts of vitamin E, required to facilitate blood flow to your scalp and promote faster growth of hair. Vitamin E aids in oxygen uptake and also boosts the circulation of blood, to trigger hair growth. Sunflower also packs calcium, zinc, omega 3 fatty acids, iron, magnesium, potassium, B vitamins, proteins and zinc; which all aids in faster healthy growth. Eat them raw, mix with dishes or eat in steamed vegetable in moderation, as they contain calories.

If sunflower is not your thing, try out pumpkin seeds as they are rich in omega-3 fatty acids, biotin, zinc and vitamins A, E and K. These seeds also contain oleic acid and linoleic acids, two oils that control the level of androgens in the body, hormones whore deficiency in the body is responsible for hair loss. They also contain cucurbitin, a kind of amino acid that strengthens effects of other minerals on your hair growth.

Whole Grains And Brown Rice

Grains like oats, barley, bajra, ragi, broken wheat and buck wheat and are rich in minerals such as iron, vitamin B and Zinc, which are good for hair follicles.

Whole grains also help in monitoring process in hormones thus contributes directly on the thickness and rate of hair growth. Whole grains are good for both protection of existing hair and growth of new hair. Add in some brown rice that has ample zinc deposits, which stimulates fast hair growth.

Green Tea And Dark Chocolate

As a favorite food to majority of people, chocolate is rich in antioxidants, Vitamin B and iron to complement the sweet taste. The dark variety of chocolate is particularly important in facilitating fast and healthy growth of hair.

Green tea, on the other hand, is beneficial in facilitating growth of hair, as it helps fight dandruff to improve the functioning of the scalp. Green tea also contains polyphenols, which assist in keeping your scalp healthy. Apart of drinking green tea, you can directly apply the tea onto the scalp to trigger hair growth.

While there's a lot you can do in terms of dieting to reverse hair loss, there's are a few foods that can greatly slow you down and water-down all the gains you've made. Sad isn't it?

Here is a list of foods you should keep away from to maintain that accelerated and constant hair growth:

Foods That Cause Hair Loss

There are a number of foods you should avoid or probably eat them in moderation if trying to grow long and healthy hair particularly within a short period of time. Most of such foods rob your body of important minerals that boost hair growth such as zinc, vitamin C, iron, omega 3 fatty acids and Calcium. Try to evade eating the following list of foods whenever possible:

1. Sugar

Avoid eating sugary food such as sweets as it can interfere with absorption of protein, an important building block of hair. As Sugar is very acidic, it can destroy B vitamins in your body and also lower concentration other minerals which directly disrupts growth of hair. Furthermore, refined carbs such as bleached flour that are low in fibre and high in sugar are indirectly linked to hair loss. Foods made from refined carbohydrates reduce your body's ability to fight stress, a major factor that lead to hair loss. Stress-related hair loss is referred to as Telogen Effluvium, a physiological stress disorder that result into shedding or thinning of hair. You should regulate intake of *sugary cereals* and processed carbs and instead go for natural sugar substitutes like honey or stevia.

2. Food Additives

Loss of hair and stunted growth of hair can be brought about by a number of synthetic additives such as caramel color, mostly processed through ammonia, sulphite or other caustic chemicals. A few natural additives such as carmine dye extract that is obtained from dried bugs and used in yoghurt, sweets and fruits drinks are also dangerous to your hair. Carmine dye causes hair loss together with lethal allergic reactions that could affect people seriously.

3. Fried Foods

Another category of foods to avoid is those containing high levels of fats, the fried foods and any solid fats or hydrogenated oils. Eating high amounts of saturated and monounsaturated fats can raise the level of Dihydrotestosterone (or DHT), a sex steroid and hormone that can hinder hair growth. Particularly in men, DHT increases testosterone levels and such increase is believed to cause *androgenic alopecia* (male pattern baldness). According to statistics from 50 million men and 30 million women in US suffer hair loss due attributed to hormonal and *androgenic alopecia* related genes. Consuming hydrogenated oils suppress the important fatty acids that your hair requires to grow hair faster.

4. Alcohol and Soft Drinks

Alcohol consumption is an enemy to growing long and healthy hair as it lowers the level of zinc, vitamin B and C and folic acid form your cells. Deficiency of these minerals leads to weak hair, slow growth and loss of hair. In addition, soft drinks such as soda contain high amounts of sweeteners, food coloring, high fructose corn syrup and processed sugars. These additives do not benefit your hair in any way, but instead lead to dry and stunted hair growth. Carbonated drinks are also high in artificial sugar which triggers insulin resistance, a disorder where body cells do not respond to hormonal insulin. According to research, baldness is one marker of insulin resistance and a signal for high blood sugar levels. To reduce hair loss, thinning and stunted growth, cut down the amounts of soft or carbonated drinks you consume.

5. Greasy Foods

Such foods lead to clogging of your arteries and also formation of greasy skin on your scalp. The greasy skin forms on the scalp lead to slow blood flow and clogging of hair follicles and sweat pores. With this restriction, DHT hormone is trapped in and thus with time you're at a risk of baldness. Though doing a shampoo may wash some of the grease, dieting on non-grease foods such as natural fats and oils is the most effective measure. Furthermore, avoid foods such as popcorn, fries or other prepackaged dishes since they are added with extra salts which are unhealthy for your body and hair growth. Be aware that excess sodium often leads to loss of hair, so maintain an intake of 2300 mg of sodium daily.

6. Processed dairy

High fat and processed daily is dangerous for your hair since its digestion produces an acidic environment in the body, and can also lead to allergic reactions. Pasteurized dairy kills the natural enzyme occurring in milk, which main role is to assist in digestion of milk. Without this enzyme, milk taken into the body doesn't benefit the cells as it's instead digested through harmful bacteria which cause buildup of toxins in the blood. By-products of processed dairy result into clogging of the skin pores, which causes epidermis plague to buildup on the scalp and trigger hair loss. To reverse hair loss and encourage growth of strong and long natural hair, only consume unpasteurized and unsweetened milk.

Topical Treatments

1: Employ Essential Oils Combined With A Scalp Massage

A scalp massage usually promotes good circulation of blood in the scalp thus keeping your hair follicles healthy and productive. For this reason, it means that it is vital for you to massage your scalp regularly for a couple of minutes to ensure. This would in turn cause proper and healthy growth of hair without necessarily losing any. To enhance the massage on your scalp, you should use a few drops of lavender or bay essential oils in an almond or sesame oil base on your scalp. These oils normally provide your hair with all the nutrients they deserve thus ensuring they grow and develop in a healthy manner without showing up any signs of hair loss.

2: Apply Hot Oil Treatment

You can use any of the natural oils including safflower, canola or olive oil to treat your hair. This is because these natural oils are usually rich in moisture that is actually a primary requirement of healthy hair. To ensure that you restore the moisture of your hair through hot oil treatment method, you should heat up the oil so that it is warm but not very hot. Then you can massage the oil gently on your scalp and then put on a shower cap for not less than one hour. When one hour is over, remove the cap and rinse or shampoo out the oil for better results. This actually feeds your hair with enough moisture that actually serves a great role in ensuring that there is minimal or no hair loss.

3: Try Rubbing Your Scalp With Garlic Juice Or Ginger Juice.

Garlic juice is mainly very important in general protection of the hair. It is mainly rich in compounds such as allicin, zinc, calcium and sulphur that usually have great health benefits, beauty advantages as well as antibiotic and antifungal properties. It is as well a rich source of mineral called selenium that is well known to fight cancer and works with vitamin E in the body to boost its antioxidant power. Moreover, the juice together with ginger and onion juice acts as blood thinners due to their salicylate content. This generally enables proper and effective blood circulation in the scalp as well as enhancing the circulatory system health. Additionally, proper flow of blood ensures that the follicles and hair cells are fed well thus reducing chances of hair loss that results due to inflammations and death of hair cells and hair follicles.

4: Try Rubbing Your Hair With Rangoli Henna

Rangoli henna is usually a natural remedy that is used to treat hair loss. It is also important for maintaining healthy hair as it usually repairs and seals the cuticle thus helping in healing hair shafts. This in turn prevents hair breakage and retains the shine of the hair. Moreover, it also adds moisture to the hair making it soft and flexible; thus reducing hair loss. It also serves to balance the pH of the scalp; this is very helpful in maintaining and preventing hair loss and prevents premature hair fall. Henna cures most problems that are generally associated with the scalp like dandruff and dryness thus ensuring healthy growth of hair. It also stops premature graying of hair as well as reversing the effects of pollution on hair and hair dryness that normally result due to excessive blow-drying. Rangoli henna also gives your hair a sleek and shiny look making it a great herbal conditioner.

5: Rub Green Tea In Your Hair

Green tea is important to your hair especially if you are experiencing hair loss. This is because it usually contains an antioxidant that serves to help healthy hair growth as well as preventing hair loss. When you are applying this, you need to follow the procedure stipulated for you to realize better results on your hair. You need to brew two bags of green tea in one cup of water and let the tea to cool slightly. When it has slightly cooled, apply it to your hair and leave the tea on for one hour. Then rinse or shampoo your hair thoroughly. This procedure assures you of better results as the green tea is actually a natural cure of hair loss. Besides this, it is a good hair conditioner that leaves your hair well moisturized thus ensuring that there is less premature hair fall as well as hair dehydration that could pose negative effects to your hair.

6: Apply Liquid Product Of Boiled Potatoes And Rosemary

Boil rosemary and potatoes and strain the liquid. Use the liquid to scrub your hair now and then. This product of boiled potatoes and rosemary is quite useful to your hair as it normally counteracts hair thinning and stimulates the growth of your hair. The scrubbing should be done using a bristle brush. This liquid product is also helpful to the scalp as it ensures that no bacteria or other microorganisms develop in the scalp. In other words, the product is antifungal as well as antibiotic. Moreover, this material encourages smooth blood flow, which actually floods hair follicles with blood thus inducing nutrients to the growing hair cells.

7: Apply Coconut Milk To Your Hair

Coconut actually provides a host of ingredients that are natural hair conditioners that promote hair growth. Coconut milk contains proteins, minerals and some essential fats that are actually very vital for your hair. Using coconut mild to treat your hair ensures that you protect your hair against breakage as well as premature fall. This milk as well carries ingredients that help to make your hair stronger right from the root. This serves to ensure that your hair is firm thus avoiding hair loss especially resulting from combing your hair or washing. Additionally, the milk from this fruit helps in enhancing blood circulation in the scalp thus ensuring that hair cells and hair follicles are fed with blood to make them active and productive thus preventing chances of hair loss.

Here is how you can make different hair care products:

Leave-in Conditioner Spray:

What you'll need

Few drops of lavender oil

1tsp of vitamin E oil (optional)

1 cup distilled water

1/2 cup Coconut Milk

How to make

1. Combine the above ingredients in a mixing bowl and stir completely until well blended.

2. Once blended, transfer to a spray bottle and then spray the mixture all over your hair.

This conditioner should leave your hair soft, shiny, moisturized and also heal any hair problems.

8: Coconut Oil For Your Hair

Apart from coconut milk, coconut oil is effective at shielding hair proteins, due to the presence of Lauric acid. This acid constitutes to the protective power of Lauric acid, a type of fatty acid that assists to bind hair proteins. This effect is useful in protecting your hair roots and stopping any possible damage. Other moisturizing hair products often fail to deliver the expected results as they don't contain the binding agent for hair protein.

In addition to that, coconut oil is rich in nutrients among them vitamin E, K as well as iron. The vitamins and minerals present in the oil helps to restore and maintain your hair's shine and softness. The presence of vitamin E helps in fighting hair problems such as dandruff, which causes hindered hair growth or hair fall. Though nutrients can be absorbed through diet, the minerals and vitamins in coconut oil get to the blood stream after being absorbed through the scalp.

You can adopt coconut oil as your routine hair care product to moisturize, heal and restore that luster or shine. The end result will be an added shine, smoother hair and a good boost to the rate of hair growth.

Here are various ways through-which you can use coconut oil for hair care:

Deep Conditioner & Hot Oil Treatment

Serves: about 7 to 8 ounces

Ingredients

15-20 drops tea tree oil

4 tablespoons jojoba oil

8 tablespoons coconut oil

Instructions

Directions

1. In a mixing bowl, stir 8 tablespoons of coconut oil until it turns smooth and of silky consistency. Whisk in tea tree oil and beat until well incorporated. Alternatively, you can use an electric mixer in place of a whisk.

2. As soon as the contents are fully combined, transfer the mixture in re-sealable containers, preferably two 4-ounce mason jars.

3. You can make small or large batches using 1 part jojoba oil to 2 parts coconut oil and a few drops of tea tree oil per each batch. You can also try extra virgin olive oil and grape-seed oil in place of jojoba oil; or argan oil except for its high cost.

4. For deep conditioning, slather on wet or damp hair and allow it to rest for around 3-5 minutes. Then use natural shampoo and condition it as usual.

5. To do hot oil treatment, slather on the wet hair and then use a hot towel straight from the dryer to cover the hair. You can also pop on a shower cap and then heat the hair using the blow dryer. Allow it to sit for around 15 minutes and then shampoo and condition as required.

Coconut Oil and Honey Hair Mask

What you'll need:

Shower Cap (optional)

Towel

Spoon

Mixing Bowl

Sauce Pan

1 tablespoon organic raw honey

1 tablespoon organic coconut oil

How to make

1. In a mixing bowl, measure equal portions of organic raw honey and organic coconut oil, or use more depending on your preferences.

2. Combine the ingredients fully to make an effective honey mask that can help open hair follicles. Then heat this mixture onto a stovetop inside a small sauce pan.

3. You can apply the mask either to wet or dry hair, but it works best on wet hair. Cover your neck and clothes using a towel and then gently apply the hair mask.

4. Sub-divide the hair into portions and then apply generous amounts from top to bottom, paying more focus on where there's hair damage.

5. Use a bun to wrap your hair and allow the mask to absorb for 30-40 minutes.

6. Once done, use regular shampoo and conditioner to wash the mask to achieve the healthy, smooth and soft hair.

Coconut Hair Cream

What you'll need

Few drops of essential oil

1 teaspoon of olive oil

2tablespoon coconut oil

How to make

1. Combine the ingredients fully in a bowl until fully blended.

2. Once done, apply to your scalp together with the strands

3. You can use the hair ream like other deep conditioners, and then let it stay for around 30-45 minutes.

Whipped Coconut Oil for Natural Hair

What you need:

1 cup coconut oil

Few drops of your favorite essential oils

How to make

1. Combine the ingredients in a mixing bowl without melting the coconut oil at first. The oil whips best when it's in solid state, or in lower than room temperature.

2. Combine on high speed using a wire whisk for around 6-7 minutes or until you obtain a light substance with airy consistency.

3. In a glass jar, spoon the whipped coconut oil and then cover lightly. Keep in a cool place, preferably in a fridge if the house is warm to avoid melting the oil. The whipped oil should stay soft even at lower temperatures.

Homemade Dandruff Treatment

What you'll need

1 tablespoon of lemon juice or fenugreek seeds

5 tablespoon of coconut oil

Essential oils of choice

How to make

1. If using a tablespoon of fenugreek seeds, crush them into powder to obtain the anti-fungus property they possess. For lemon, extract a tablespoon of lemon juice from a fresh fruit.

2. Measure about 5 tablespoons of coconut oil and warm it briefly, and then add a tablespoon of lemon juice or fenugreek powder into the warm oil.

3. Combine the ingredients until well incorporated and then apply carefully onto your scalp. Just massage it and allow it to soak for around 20-30 minutes.

4. Use your natural shampoo to wash it off to eliminate the dandruff. Then use a warm towel to cover the hair.

As you can clearly see, coconut oil is an effective product for conditioning, repairing damaged hair and maintaining healthy hair. However, when buying coconut oil products, you should avoid those made of refined coconut oil but instead go for extra virgin coconut oil. The unrefined coconut oil has all the active substances intact and thus is more effective than the processed counterpart.

9: Lemon for Hair Care

Did you know that lemon is one of the natural resources that can be reliable in restoring and maintaining healthy looking hair?

Actually, using the lemon can make your hair strong and dense and will effectively combat the occurrence of baldness or hair loss for that matter. The reason why it's suitable in hair care is that lemon contains vitamin C or ascorbic acid that that is effective in preventing hair loss. Lemon juice also has excellent bleaching properties that have been used in other fields such as bleaching fabrics and therefore you can rely on if for similar results in bleaching hair.

The ascorbic acid found in lemon in the presence of sunlight usually get oxidized making its application on the hair bring a bleaching effect. The treatment is significantly effective in lightening your hair leaving it soft but resistant to breakage.

Applying lemon juice to the scalp can help treat a number of hair problems such as hair loss, dandruff, discoloring and treating smelly hair. Lemon is excellent source of phosphorous and vitamins B and C needed to fight against occurrence of dandruff and baldness.

Lemon helps strengthen your hair roots as well as minimizing secretion of oils into the scalp. Your body can secrete excessive, sebum, which makes the hair follicles clogged affecting the health of the hair. An oily scalp cannot allow hair to grow on it naturally and therefore lemon juice can help a lot in correcting the condition.

Lemon is also a recommendable conditioning hair rinse in that produces a pH balanced, shiny and healthy hair. Coupled with vinegar for homemade conditioning, the treatment will help you maintain a greasy scalp and the under control. This will solve many issues as well improving the appearance of your dull hair. Lemon also fights scalp infections and kill germs, and minimizes the side effects of using chemical hair products that most people use. This will make your hair shiny with a lighter healthier look.

Here are a few applications of lemon as far as hair care is concerned:

Treating hair loss

-To make a hair treatment solution, cut the lemon into fine pieces and then rub into your hair and allow it to stand overnight when still wrapped with a towel. Do this treatment 3 times a week, and you will see the effectiveness of the lemon juice.

-You can also treat hair loss by crushing the lemon seeds together with black pepper and forming a paste or by mixing one part vinegar with one part lemon juice. Apply the vinegar mixture to the scalp for 10 minutes and allow the mixture to work in 10 minutes. This treatment is also very production in minimizing hair loss.

-You can also mix equal amounts of lemon and coconut water to make a healthy solution to treat your hair. The extract will nourish the hair as it also treats and prevent further hair loss.

Treating dandruff

Dandruff can be defined as a scalp crust or where the dead skin rests and will interrupt development of health hair. Or in simpler terms, it's the small pieces of dead skin that occur in the hair, resulting from hair damage.

A more common cause of hair loss is the scratching of the scalp which will break and weaken the hair and eventually lead to hair loss.

-Lemon juice is effective in eliminating the dead skin from the scalp where the treatment involves performing 2-3 times per week routine treatment. Rub lemon juice into the hair or the scalp and wait for about 20-30 minutes to dry. Once dry, rinse the head thoroughly. The juice will treat the dandruff and prevent further occurrence.

-Lemon can also be used with common salt to scrub the scalp in a salted slice of lemon to treat dandruff problems. This treatment is very effective and does not result into any irritation to the scalp due to the combination with salt. You can try the treatment if you suffer from persistent oily dandruffs.

10: Apple Cider Vinegar

Also known as ACV or cider vinegar, apple cider vinegar is a pale or medium amber colored natural substance that comes from apple or cider. Vinegar has the ability to soften the skin, improve the skin tone, clear acne and reduce or treat dandruff occurring on the hair.

This ability comes from the anti-inflammatory properties of vinegar, which comes from Malic and lactic acids found in vinegar. The acids are effective for hardening the scalp, balancing the pH of hair scalp as well as treating common hard problems such as dnadruff.

These are "tens of ways" you can use ACV, particularly if you get a brand that is organic, raw, unfiltered and unpasteurized. Organically made apple cider vinegar contains the *mother of vinegar*, which is the healthiest and most beneficial part of the vinegar.

Here's how you can use vinegar on your hair:

Dandruff Treatment

ACV contains active enzymes and acids, which are effective in killing bacteria that causes hair fall, itchiness and hair flakes. The antifungal and acidic properties help balance pH of the scalp, preventing further fungal infection.

To control dandruff and help create a healthy environment for hair to thrive, just mix together two equal parts of vinegar and water and then massage into your hair before doing shampoo. You can also add a teaspoon of vinegar to the shampoo and then wash the hair, massage the hair together with the scalp.

Hair Rinse

Majority of hair care products in the market nowadays are strongly alkaline and can leave loads of toxic substances in your scalp. Apple cider vinegar contains acetic acid, which can eliminate build-up of residue from these hair care product, therefore maintaining the shiny and lustrous looks.

In this case, vinegar works by closing the cuticles of your hair, making light shine on the hair for that shiny apperance.

To "detoxify" your hair from buildup of chemicals, simply combine about 2 tablespoons of ACV and add to a cup of water. Use this apple cider mixture to douche the hair after ordinary washing. Alternatively, you can mix one part of water to one part ACV, and then pour this mixture to your hair after shampooing. You should allow the hair to condition fully for a few minutes, and then rinse with water.

To Cure Black Heads

Vinegar is an effective remedy for blackheads, a condition that is characterized by plugs of sebum into the hair follicle, that's darkened from oxidation process. To cure naturally eliminate blackheads, add a tablespoon of apple cider vinegar to 3 mashed straw berries, and allow this mixture to sit for 2 hours. Now strain the mixture and then apply the juice onto the oily areas of your hair and leave it overnight. This treatment is very effective in gradual reduction of black heads.

Treat hair loss

Balding is an embarrassing situation that can hamper your efforts to main healthy and beautiful hair, thereby lowering your self-esteem. To curb this problem, just mix 1 teaspoon of cayenne powder to a tablespoon of apple cider vinegar and apply the mixture to your scalp. Allow this mixture to remain for 30 minutes and then use water to rinse your hair.

Remedy for razor bump

A razor bump or burn is caused by a razor defect during shaving, such as lack of required sharpness or other infections. Apple cider vinegar is important for soothing irritated skin as well as helping the ingrown hairs to develop more easily. The acetic acids in the vinegar constitutes to the anti-inflammatory power of vinegar. To treat razor bumps, moisten a piece of cotton ball with undiluted vinegar, and then swipe it over the affected area. In case you have aggravated pumps, apply a light layer of honey to this area, allow to rest for about 5 minutes and then rinse. When thoroughly clean, pat dry and then apply the undiluted vinegar with the cotton ball.

Cure for itchy scalp

On top of treating dandruff, ACV is also effective in soothing an itching scalp, while still triggering the hair follicles to generate healthy hair. This is because vinegar has alpha hydroxyl acids, effective for exfoliating the top layers of the skin. This effect exposes the smoother and softer skin below the infected skin. To sooth your itching scalp, mix 1-2 parts of water with one part of vinegar and then saturate it on the skin for 10 minutes daily.

11: Massaging Your Scalp With Castor Oil

One way of growing healthy hair naturally is to massage the scalp with cold-pressed castor oil. This oil has high viscosity thus should coat the hair and inhibit possible hair fall which lead to hair loss.

Castor oil is also rich in fatty acids and vitamin E which both enhance hair growth.

Here's how you can do that once you obtain cold-pressed version of the oil:

-Mix together an equal amount of castor oil and coconut oil and gently heat to melt. Castor oil can be used alone but coconut oil makes it less thick.

-Apply this mixture onto the scalp and hair and gently massage in circular motions. Then comb the hair to allow the oil reach all hair and eliminate tangles.

-Use a towel that has been moistened with warm water to cover the hair and allow the castor oil to soak for more than an hour.

-Once done, shampoo with a natural produce and follow this treatment once per week for thicker and longer hair.

12: Use Indian Gooseberry

This fruit is an antioxidant, anti-inflammatory and also antibacterial; and is an effective exfoliating agent. By helping remove dead layers of cells from your scalp, Indian gooseberry assists to maintain a healthy scalp and better hair growth rate.

Follow these steps to treat your scalp with Indian gooseberry:

-Combine a tablespoon of the gooseberry with 2 tablespoons of coconut oil and heat to a boil.

-Then strain the oil from gooseberry and gently massage on the scalp at night. (Do this each and every night before sleeping).

-The next day, shampoo hair as usual. You should do this treatment with Indian gooseberry once every week.

-Alternatively, you can also combine ½ cup of gooseberry powder with a ¼ cup of warm water and allow it rest for 10-15 minutes.

-Now apply the gooseberry paste onto the hair and let it soak for 20 minutes and then rinse it off. In this case however, do not shampoo the hair immediately but allow a few hours for the treatment to work.

-Repeat this gooseberry paste treatment after a couple of weeks. Be aware that Indian gooseberry can also be eaten but if you can't get the actual fruit, go for its extract that's sold as dietary supplement.

13: Use Avocado to Naturally Thicken Hair

To grow new, healthy and thicker hair, you can use avocado paste particularly with added vitamin E, which is needed for healthy hair shaft.

-Simply mix together a tablespoon of olive oil with mashed banana and mashed avocado to make a paste

-Apply this to the scalp and let the mixture soak for 30 minutes for nutrients to get to your scalp. Once done, ensure you shampoo the hair.

-A ½ ripe avocado can also be combined with 2 tablespoons of wheat germ oil to make a hydrating hair mask. Apply the mask after shampooing and then let the treatment work for 20-30 minutes before washing off.

-Then rinse the hair and shampoo it a second time. Use this mask regularly, preferably once per week.

14: Egg yolks and Egg Oil Treatment

Egg is rich in Docosahexaenoic Acid (commonly referred to as DHA), a long-chain polyunsaturated omega-3 fatty acid. DNA is useful in nourishing the follicle cells while the cholesterol in eggs fights dandruff and brings luster and shine onto hair.

Long term of egg yolk can help prevent dandruff from reoccurring and encourage growth of thick and healthy hair. Treating your scalp with eggs is an effective way to fight hair-loss related problems only that you might be left with a mild egg smell.

-Combine yolks from 1-2 eggs in a bowl

-Apply the egg yolk on a dry head ensuring to only touch the scalp area.

-Then put a plastic bag over your scalp to prevent leaking or extreme smell

-Allow the treatment to work for approximately 1 hour and then shampoo your hair to completely wash out the eggs.

-To remove any resultant egg smell, wash the hair twice with mild shampoo

If you find egg yolk treatment somewhat messy, consider washing it with egg oil (Eyova). Egg oil is better than yolk masks since it doesn't smell or "cook in your hair" during hot shower.

-Obtain sufficient amount of egg oil and massage it into your scalp for 5-10 minutes or preferably overnight.

-Then shampoo using a mild herbal shampoo in the morning

- You should only shampoo once, as overdoing the shampoo can eat away the natural lipids from your hair and scalp and cause it to become dry and brittle.

Egg oil is effective when used about 2-3 times every week for a period of 12 weeks, as this offer the necessary revitalizing of follicular cell membranes.

15: Use Seeds to Fight Hair Loss

Various seeds such as fenugreek, flaxseed and cumin seeds are useful in combating hair loss and enhancing hair growth. For instance, flaxseeds have high amounts of omega 3 fatty acids and proteins that help boost growth of healthy and thicker hair. Cumin seeds and fenugreek seeds are rich in many vitamins and nutrients that help restore healthy and strong hair.

Here's how you can ease each of the seeds individually for natural hair growth:

- ***Fenugreek***

-Soak 1-2 tablespoons of these seeds in water for about 8-10 hours

-Once set, grind them to make a smooth paste and then add in 2 teaspoons of coconut milk.

-Gently apply this mixture on the hair and scalp and let it sit for around 30 minutes.

-Then wash with lukewarm water and repeat the treatment weekly to enhance thick hair and to prevent dry scalp

- Alternatively, you can soak the seeds in water preferably overnight and then use the resulting mixture as your hair rinse.

-Treat the hair 1-2 times per week with fenugreek seeds to help eliminate dandruff and encourage growth of healthy hair.

- ***Flaxseed***

-Soak ¼ cup of flaxseeds in water overnight and then boil in 2 cups of water on high heat while stirring now and again.

-When the mixture becomes thick with a foamy jelly appearance, remove from heat and strain the gel.

-If necessary, consider adding your favorite essential oil such as peppermint or lavender and let it cool before using it as a regular hair gel.

-The flaxseed gel is suited for wavy and curly hair. Good for you, you can also consume flaxseeds in their natural form or even its oily foam to help promote growth of shiny and thicker hair.

- ***Cumin Seeds***

-Just soak the cumin seeds into castor or olive oil and allow to absorb overnight.

-The next day, apply this mixture to the hair and later wash after 15-20 minutes using a mild shampoo.

16: Exfoliating with Baking Soda

This mild exfoliant is effective in removing dead skin cells and absorbing extra oil from the scalp. Baking soda also help balance pH levels on the scalp and control the growth of fungi that lead to dandruff and hair loss. Due to its tiny particles, it's able to eliminate the loose flakes that are stuck into the hair as opposed to other anti-dandruff agents that just break it into pieces. To use baking soda for hair loss and dandruff treatment, follow these steps:

-Dampen your hair and then rub some baking soda onto the scalp

-Wait for 5-10 minutes and then use warm water to rinse the hair completely

-Apply this treatment about 2 times weekly for a number of weeks. However, you shouldn't shampoo the hair after treating with baking soda.

17: Reetha Or Soap Nuts Treatment

This traditional Indian cure dandruff also promotes growth of strong and long hair. Soap nuts are rich in anti-bacterial properties that help solve scalp problems and restore healthy, shiny and thick hair. You only need about 10-15 soap nuts, 2-3 cups of water and a tablespoon of Amla powder or juice:

-Begin by soaking the soap nuts in water, preferably overnight

-The following day, just grind the nuts and then boil their powder in water

-Strain to obtain soap nuts mixture, to which you add amla powder or juice and combine completely

-If necessary, add in some water to create some kind of paste

-Apply the mixture on your scalp, waiting for about 15 to 30 minutes and then use a mild shampoo to rinse the hair.

18: Yogurt and Pepper Treament

Yeast is one of the agents responsible for inflammation, a situation that leads to accumulation of yeast, dandruff and hairloss. Yoghurt is a good remedy for improving the number of friendly bacteria living in the body. It's also anti-scaling agent which combines with anti-fungal pepper works wonders to fight dandruff and hair loss.

-Obtain 2 teaspoons of black pepper and grind to fineness

-Add about a cup of fresh yoghurt or curd into the pepper and stir well

-Once combined well, gently apply to the scalp, ensuring to only touch the scalp but not the hair.

-Let the scalp rest undisturbed for about 1 hour and then do a rinse, followed by a mild shampoo.

19: Indian Lilac/Neem

Indian lilac is known for its antibacterial anti-inflammatory and antifungal properties. The herb has shown its ability to fight dandruff and related problems such as acnes on scalp, hair loss and itchy scalp.

-Simply boil a handful of Indian lilac in about 4 cups of water

-Once done, cool the hot mixture for a few minutes and then strain and discard any solid parts

-Use this mixture as your hair rinse; then leave it undisturbed for around 30 minutes before you rinse off with water

-Repeat this treatment about 2-3 times per week.

20: Tree Oil For Natural Hair Growth

Oils such as tea tree and olive are useful in removing extra sebum on your scalp, keeping dandruff in control and encouraging hair growth. The oil from tea tree is a strong anti-fungicide and has healing properties to sooth and repair itchy or sore skin. To treat your hair or scalp, first obtain a tablespoon of tea tree oil and a cup of water alongside a squirt bottle.

-Then pour a tablespoon of tea tree oil into warm water placed in a squirt bottle and shake properly.

-Shampoo your hair as usual and then spray this mixture onto the scalp, massage it and allow the treatment to work for 10-15 minutes.

-To clean out tea tree oil remnants from your scalp, pat dry with a dump towel.

Note: You should only use tea tree oil for topical application, which means that you avoid ingesting or swallowing the oil.

Lifestyle Changes

Take great care of the hair you have

You need to greatly take care of your hair to ensure that you do not cause your own hair loss. The best way you can avoid this is by totally avoiding brushing your wet hair as this is likely to get loose the hair thus contributing to hair loss. You should as well avoid rubbing hair dry with a towel as the friction that arises between the hair and the rough towel affects your hair in great depths. Additionally, you need to let you hair dry or else blow dry it to the point of dampness and then let it dry from there gradually. This is very important as it serves to ensure that moisture is as well retained in your hair thus avoiding a case where it extremely dries until it becomes subject to hair loss.

Reduce stress

Stress is known to be a huge contributor to hair loss. This means that we need to practice all things that can really help us manage our stress if we want to be healthy. For you to overcome stress, you need to do a number of things that have been proved and tested to counter the effects of stress. One way you can overcome stress is by practicing meditation. Meditation normally helps to reduce your stress and to restore your hormonal balance and this helps to enhance the blood circulation through the scalp thus enhancing the productivity of the follicles and hair cells. This helps to ensure that there are less chances of hair falling prematurely. Levels of stress can as well be lowered by doing a bit of exercise such as walking or cycling or you can engage yourself in playing games such as tennis or football as they would help to take out your aggression. Whenever you feel like you are stressed, you can talk or write it down. Converse with your spouse, a friend, relatives, or even talk to a therapist about what you are experiencing, as they can be help you to relieve your stress. If you have no one around you, you can proceed and write or record your feelings and experiences in a journal as it can be helpful while trying to trace causes of you stress.

Preventive Oils

Olive oil

Olive oil has several properties that are important for your hair. It is an excellent conditioner and has a nourishing effect on your hair, as it is able to penetrate the hair shaft much more effectively than other oils. It also has moisturizing properties, and this helps to keep your hair moisturized and flexible thus preventing hair breakage. Moreover, this oil is rich in vitamin E and monounsaturated fatty acids that play an important role in promoting growth of healthy hair. The vitamins available in this oil as well play great role in maintaining the activity of hair cells and hair follicle thus avoiding premature hair fall.

Almond oil

Almond oil is actually very effective when it comes to hair care because of its emollient or softening action. It makes your hair smooth and soft thus ensuring that there is less hair breakage or hair fall. It is also rich in vitamins D and E as well as minerals such as calcium and magnesium that are very helpful in hair growth. Due to this reason, almond oil acts as a natural moisturizer for your hair thus preventing it from turning dry and brittle, which could lead to hair loss. You should thus treat or rub your hair with almond oil care to help maintain your healthy hair as well prevent your hair from loss that could lead to baldness.

Lavender oil

This oil is actually very helpful to your hair because of its calming and relaxing properties. It is usually highly effective in dealing with nits and lice that could affect the health your hair leading to hair loss. Massaging lavender oil into your scalp is quite vital as this oil also increases blood circulation in the scalp thus enabling provision of nutrients to hair cells and follicles, which makes sure that they remain active for healthy hair.

Castor oil

Castor oil usually has excellent hair growth-promoting properties when applied externally to the hair. For this reason, it is also considered an effective remedy for hair thinning. The benefits of the oil are generally due to its ingredients ricinoleic acid that normally has antifungal, antibacterial as well as anti-inflammatory properties that are quite vital for your hair cells and the scalp in general. The oil is also rich in vitamin E that normally has antioxidant action thus very important to your hair.

Carrot essential oil

This natural oil is a thick and orange paste that you can obtain either in its pure form and dilute or buy as a ready to use extract. Carrot essential oil doubles as both skincare and hair care emulsion due to the high quality of antioxidants and carotene. The oil can also help you to grow hair especially if faced by baldness. Application of this essential oil can solve a number of perennial problems associated with hair. Furthermore, you can also reach for carrot seed essential oil which is slightly different from carrot root oil and has got its uniqueness too. The oil is important for offering rejuvenating power especially when combined with carrot root oil for better results.

Ylang Ylang essential oil

This essential oil is useful in treating oily hair, a condition caused by overproduction of the natural hair oils. The oil is also good for treating dandruff, a common chronic scalp condition characterized by flaking of the skin on your scalp. On the same note, Ylang Ylang oil is an excellent antiseptic that can kill bacteria and viruses affecting your hair cells, to promote growth of new hair. Furthermore, the essential oil is important in stimulating blood flow into the scalp as well as strengthening the scalp to help with hair loss.

Cedar-wood essential oil

This essential oil from cedar wood is important in moisturizing and treating dry and oily scalp on top of stimulating the scalp and hair follicles. In case you suffer baldness, cedar wood essential oil is important in treating hair loss and dandruff. Furthermore, cedar-wood is an antiseptic and an astringent, which means it can help protect the scalp and to minimize bleeding caused by minor abrasions.

How To Use Preventive Oils For Hair Care

In order to effectively massage hair and possibly avoid any allergic reaction, try keeping the base oil as light as possible. To do so, dilute these natural oils with carrier oils such apricot kernel, peach kernel, grape-seed and jojoba oil.

If your hair is thick and coarse hair, try using rich nourishing oils like avocado, olive, hemp, rose hip, evening primrose and sesame oils. Ensure that you make a balanced hydrating agent by combining good quantities of natural and corresponding carrier oils.

For instance, use 3-5 drops of preventive oil with a teaspoon or 5 ml of the base oil like jojoba oil.

Once you have diluted preventive oils, massage it onto your hair and scalp, and allow it to soak for at least 1 hour or overnight. Then wash with your natural shampoo and allow the hair to dry naturally.

For hair rinse, use 10-20 drops of these oils into the final rinse or herbal rinse. This should help boost the condition of the hair and scalp. Try adding a few drops of homemade shampoo to increase the potency of the hair rinse. Be aware that natural oils normally evaporate quickly and thus shouldn't be left exposed.

On top of using topical treatments and essential oils to reverse hair loss, did you know that how you treat your hair matters? Let's see ways in which you can care for your hair to avoid possible hair loss:

Ways of Caring for Your Hair Naturally

1. Style hair in moderation

Frequent styling of hair can slow down the growth rate of your hair and also lead to hair loss. Cleaning the hair in harsh ways also causes damage, thinning and loss of hair, which all hinders faster growth of hair. Though the hair damage may be reversible, it causes slow hair growth and a lot of time to restore the natural hair health.

2. Avoid hair treatment

Try to avoid frequent bleaching, curling, mechanical straightening, crimping or perming as such treatments weaken your hair strands and lead to breakage of hair. Using of hot tools to style hair can also damage your hair, so only do manual or air drying to conserve your hair. Apply oils on hair ends before styling with heat tools to make ends healthy.

3. Choose hair products carefully

Look for ingredients included in a hair product you're buying and then research on possible side effects it might cause. Also, you can try a number of hair products and evaluate the one that works perfect for you.

Choose hair products that clean hair well and facilitate continuous hair growth, lower hair breakage or hair loss. Look for products with natural oils like jojoba, olive, almond, avocado and coconut, which assist reduce hair breakage and hair loss.

4. Avoid harsh hair styles

A number of hair styles such as tight ponytails and cornrows pull your hair tightly, and thus exert some stress on the hair follicles to cause damage.

When hairdressing, look for better styles that do not pull tight on your roots, as you moderate chemical treatments and hot styling of your hair. Also avoid using rubber bands to hold hair back as this can snug the hair and cause breakages.

5. Comb hair twice daily

Hair treatments such as excessive combing or brushing the hair may pull out your hair prematurely, thus hindering fast hair growth.

Do not pull your hair harshly or detangle it while not using a hair conditioner or a detangling spray. While combing or brushing long hair, hold it on one hand as you style to avoid pulling off hair from its root.

6. Don't shampoo after each shower

It's important to skip shampoo after washing the hair as opposed to hair conditioner. Hair shampoo is meant to remove any dirt and accumulation of toxins from the scalp, but might also wash away the natural oils from strands.

The oils help keep the strands healthy and soft and thus regular shampooing dries and damage hair. When you shampoo hair, be gentle and ensure to only lather up at the scalp. Then allow the suds to slide down your hair strands, to hit the entire hair as you rinse with cold water.

7. Care for hair while asleep

Do not sleep with a tight braid or tight pony tail as these don't allow fast growth of hair, and might lead to hair breakage and scalp pains. Thus, get a loose braid or ponytail instead, and try to sleep on a silk pillow case. As opposed to cotton covers, silk doesn't cause friction and is gentler to the hair. A silk pillowcase can enable you to fight facial wrinkles that appear on the skin around the face.

8. Rinse with cold water

After shower, rinse the hair with cold water to facilitate healthy growth and maintenance of long hair for longer. Cold water can lay your hair's outer layer smoother and thus inhibit heat damage, snags and moisture loss. To rinse, just do it for a few seconds but in a thorough way to help make hair more natural and healthy.

Medical Assistance

Use drugs

If you notice that you are experiencing hair loss, it would be better that you get medical help. This will actually help you in getting drugs such as propecia and Rogaine that are FDA approved for treating hair loss. These drugs help greatly as they actually inhibit the thinning of hair and increase the coverage of the scalp. Propecia mainly helps achieve this by inhibiting conversion of testosterone into dihydrotestosterone, a hormone that normally shrinks the hair follicles thus causing hair loss. The Rogaine helps to stimulate the hair follicles thus allowing them to remain active and productive to prevent premature falling of hair.

Conclusion

I hope this book was able to help you to find suitable and effective ways of dealing with hair loss. Many people are struggling with hair loss problems due to different reasons. Some causes of hair loss could be due to our own lifestyle decisions, while others may be beyond our reach like in the case of genetics. As indicated above, various things cause hair loss; thus, the treatments for hair loss vary depending on the cause while some treatments can be used for treating different kinds of hair loss. Thus, you need not to lose hope when you start experiencing hair loss because you can use the treatments mentioned above to address the problem.

Now is your turn to take action by applying the specific strategies explained to enhance hair growth and prevent any more hair loss.

Do You Like My Book & Approach To Publishing?

If you like my writing and style and would love the ease of learning literally everything you can get your hands on from Fantonpublishers.com, I'd really need you to do me either of the following favors.

6 Things

I'll be honest; publishing books on what I learn in my line of work gives me satisfaction. But the biggest satisfaction that I can get as an author is knowing that I am influencing people's lives positively through the content I publish. Greater joy even comes from knowing that customers appreciate the great content that they have read in every book through giving feedback, subscribing to my newsletter, sending emails to tell me how transformative the content they read is, following me on social media and buying several of my books. That's why I am always seeking to engage my readers at a personal level to know them and for them to know me, not just as an author but as a person because we all want to belong. That's why I strive to use different channels to engage my readers so that I can ultimately build a cordial relationship with them for our mutual success i.e. I succeed as an author while at the same time my readers learn stuff that takes days and sometimes weeks to write, edit, format and publish in a matter of hours.

To build this relationship, I'd really appreciate if you could do any or all the following:

1: First, I'd Love It If You Leave a Review of This Book on Amazon.

Let me be honest; reviews play a monumental role in determining whether customers purchase different products online. From the thousands of other books that are on Amazon about the topic, you chose to read this one. I am grateful for that. I may not know why you read my book, especially until the end considering the fact that most readers don't read until the end. Perhaps you purchased this book after reading some of the reviews and were glued with reading the book because it was educative and engaging. Even if you didn't read it because of the positive reviews, perhaps you can make the next customer's purchasing decision a lot easier by posting a review of this book on Amazon!

I'd love it if you did that, as this would help me spread word out about my books and publishing business. The more the readers, the bigger a community we build and we all benefit! If you could leave your honest review of this book on Amazon, I'd be forever grateful (well, I am already grateful to you for purchasing the book and reading it until the end- I don't' take that for granted!). Please Leave a Review of This Book on Amazon.

2: Check Out My Other Books

As I stated earlier, my biggest joy in all this is building an audience that loves my approach to publishing and the amazing content I publish. I know every author has his/her style. Mine is publishing what I learn to readers out there so that they can learn what is trending, what other readers are also searching for in the nonfiction world and much more. As such, if you read the other books I have published, you will undoubtedly know a lot more than the average person on a diverse range of issues. And as you well know, knowledge is power- and the biggest investment that you can ever have on your life!

PS: If you want me to filter everything for you to include only Ketogenic diet books, you can subscribe to my newsletter and I will send you a list of all my Ketogenic diet books along with other useful content that I come across to ensure you succeed while at it http://bit.ly/2Cketodietfanton.

3: Let's Get In Touch

Let's get closer than just leaving reviews and buying my other books. Reach out to me through email, like or follow me on social media and let's interact. You will perhaps get to know stuff about me that will change your life in a way. As we interact, we will also influence each other in a way. I' definitely would love to learn something from you as we get to know each other.

Antony

Website: http://www.fantonpublishers.com/

Email: Support@fantonpublishers.com

Twitter: https://twitter.com/FantonPublisher

Facebook Page: https://www.facebook.com/Fantonpublisher/

My Ketogenic Diet Books Page: https://www.facebook.com/pg/Fast-Keto-Meals-336338180266944

Private Facebook Group For Readers: https://www.facebook.com/groups/FantonPublishers/

Pinterest: https://www.pinterest.com/fantonpublisher/

4: Grab Some Freebies On Your Way Out; Giving Is Receiving, Right?

I gave you 2 freebies at the start of the book, one on general life transformation and one about the Ketogenic diet. You are free to choose either or both!

Ketogenic Diet Freebie: http://bit.ly/2fantonpubketo

5 Pillar Life Transformation Checklist: http://bit.ly/2fantonfreebie

5: Suggest Topics That You'd Love Me To Cover To Increase Your Knowledge Bank.
As I stated, I love feedback; any type of feedback- positive or negative. As such, make sure to reach out. I am looking forward to seeing your suggestions and insights on the topic. You could even suggest improvements to this book. Simply send me a message on Support@fantonpublishers.com. As a publisher, I strive to publish content that my readers are actively looking for. Therefore, your input is highly important.

6: Subscribe To My Newsletter To Know When I Publish New Books.

I already mentioned this earlier; I love to connect with my readers. This is just another avenue for me to connect to you. As such, if you would love to know whenever I publish new books and blog posts, subscribe to my newsletter at http://bit.ly/2fantonpubnewbooks. You will be the first to know whenever I have fresh content!

My Other Books

As I already mentioned, I write books on all manner of topics. In this part of the book, I have categorized them all for easy reading. If you wish to receive notifications about a certain category of books, I have provided a link below every category to ensure you only receive what you are looking for.

Weight Loss Books

You can search for the titles on Amazon.

General Weight Loss Books

The books in this category will help you lose weight irrespective of the approach you are using i.e. dieting or workout. I recommend you have them even if you are on specific diets or using specific workouts for weight loss.

Binge Eating: Binge Eating Disorder Cure: Easy To Follow Tips For Eating Only What Your Body Needs

Lose Weight: Lose Weight Fast Naturally: How to Lose Weight Fast Without Having To Become a Gym Rat or Dieting Like a Maniac

Lose Weight: Lose Weight Permanently: Effective Strategies on How to Lose Weight Easily and Permanently

Get updates when we publish any book about weight loss: http://bit.ly/2fantonweightlossbooks

Weight Loss Books On Specific Diets

Ketogenic Diet Books

KETOGENIC DIET: Keto Diet Made Easy: Beginners Guide on How to Burn Fat Fast With the Keto Diet (Including 100+ Recipes That You Can Prepare Within 20 Minutes)- New Edition

KETOGENIC DIET: Ketogenic Diet Recipes That You Can Prepare Using 7 Ingredients and Less in Less Than 30 Minutes

Ketogenic Diet: With A Sustainable Twist: Lose Weight Rapidly With Ketogenic Diet Recipes You Can Make Within 25 Minutes

Ketogenic Diet: Keto Diet Breakfast Recipes

Get updates when we publish any book on the Ketogenic diet: http://bit.ly/2fantonpubketo

Intermittent Fasting Books

Intermittent Fasting: A Complete Beginners Guide to Intermittent Fasting For Weight Loss, Increased Energy, and A Healthy Life

Get updates when we publish any book on intermittent fasting: http://bit.ly/2fantonbooksIF

Any Other Diet

Get updates when we publish any book on any other diet that will help you to lose weight and keep it off: http://bit.ly/2fantonsdietbooks

Relationships Books

Wedding: Budget Wedding: Wedding Planning On The Cheap (Master How To Plan A Dream Wedding On Budget)

How To Get Your Ex Back: Step By Step Formula On How To Get Your Ex Back And Keep Him/her For Good

SEX POSITIONS: Sex: Unleash The Tiger In You Using These 90-Day Sex Positions With Pictures

Money Problems: How To Solve Relationship Money Problems: Save Your Marriage By Learning How To Fix All Your Money Problems And Save Your Relationship

Family Communication: A Simple Powerful Communication Strategy to Transform Your Relationship with Your Kids and Enjoy Being a Parent Again

Get updates when we publish any book that will help you improve on your personal and professional relationships: http://bit.ly/2fantonsrelations

Personal Development

Body Language: Master Body Language: A Practical Guide to Understanding Nonverbal Communication and Improving Your Relationships

Subconscious Mind: Tame, Reprogram & Control Your Subconscious Mind To Transform Your Life

Emotional Intelligence: The Mindfulness Guide To Mastering Your Emotions, Getting Ahead And Improving Your Life

Get updates when we publish any book that will help you become a better person by boosting your productivity, achieving more of your goals, beating procrastination, breaking bad habits, forming new habits, beat stress, building your self-esteem and confidence and much more: http://bit.ly/2fantonpubpersonaldevl

Personal Finance & Investing Books

Real Estate: Rental Property Investment Guide: How To Buy & Manage Rental Property For Profits

MONEY: Make Money Online: 150+ Real Ways to Make Real Money Online (Plus 50 Bonus Tips to Guarantee Your Success)

Money: How To Make Money Online: Make Money Online In 101 Ways

Get updates when we publish any book that will help you up your game in personal finance and investing: http://bit.ly/2fantonpersfinbooks

Health & Fitness Books

PMS CURE: Easy To Follow Home Remedies For PMS & PMDD

Testosterone: How to Boost Your Testosterone Levels in 15 Different Ways Naturally

Hair Loss: How to Stop Hair Loss: Actionable Steps to Stop Hair Loss (Hair Loss Cure, Hair Care, Natural Hair Loss Cures)

Hashimoto's: Hashimoto's Cookbook: Eliminate Toxins and Restore Thyroid Health through Diet In 1 Month

Stress: The Psychology of Managing Pressure: Practical Strategies to turn Pressure into Positive Energy (5 Key Stress Techniques for Stress, Anxiety, and Depression Relief)

Get updates when we publish any book that will help you up your game in health and fitness: http://bit.ly/2fantonhealthnfit

Book Summaries

This category will feature summaries of some of your favorite books, written in a manner you can easily digest and follow:

Summary: The Millionaire Next Door: The Surprising Secrets of America's Wealthy

Summary: The Plant Paradox: The Hidden Dangers In "Healthy" Foods That Cause Disease And Weight Gain

Get updates whenever we publish new book summaries: http://bit.ly/2fantons

All The Other Niches

This category of books includes anything that we cannot realistically fit in the categories above. As always, if you want just about anything you can get to read, this is the category for you!

Travel Books

Kenya: Travel Guide: The Traveler's Guide to Make The Most Out of Your Trip to Kenya (Kenya Tourists Guide)

Dog Training

Dog Tricks: 15 Tricks You Must Teach Your Dog before Anything Else

World Issues Books

ISIS/ISIL: The Rise and Rise of the Islamic State: A Comprehensive Guide on ISIS & ISIL

Get notifications when we publish books on anything else above from the niches I mentioned above: http://bit.ly/2fantonpubnewbooks

See You On The Other Side!

See, I publish books on just about any topic imaginable!

If you have any suggestions on topics you would want me to cover, feel free to get in touch:

Website: http://www.fantonpublishers.com/

Email: Support@fantonpublishers.com

Twitter: https://twitter.com/FantonPublisher

My Ketogenic Diet Books Page: https://www.facebook.com/pg/Fast-Keto-Meals-336338180266944

Facebook Page: https://www.facebook.com/Fantonpublisher/

Private Facebook Group For Readers: https://www.facebook.com/groups/FantonPublishers/

Pinterest: https://www.pinterest.com/fantonpublisher/

PS: You can subscribe to my mailing list to know when I publish new books:

Hey! This is not the entire list! You can check an updated list of all my books on:

My Author Central: amazon.com/author/fantonpublishers

My Website: http://www.fantonpublishers.com

Stay With Me On My Journey To Making Passive Income Online

I have to admit; my writing business makes several six figures a year in profits (after paying ourselves salaries). Until recently, I didn't realize just how hard we worked to build this business to what it has become so far.

However, while it is profitable and I want to do it in the long term, I understand its limitations. I know I cannot have an endless number of writers at a time especially if we are to continue delivering high quality products to our customers and readers consistently.

That's why I have recently started getting more serious with self-publishing to help me build a passive income business i.e. income that is not pegged on the number of writers and hours that we put to develop our products.

Thanks to my vast experience and dedication to get things done, I am committed to building a six figure passive income publishing business.

To make sure you are part of this journey, I am inviting you to subscribe to our newsletter (http://bit.ly/2fanton6figprogress) to know my progress as far as passive income generation is concerned. That's not all; if making passive income, just like me, is something you'd love to venture into, you can follow my 'tell it all' blog, which I explain everything I have done to promote every book and how the results are turning out with figures and images.

My goal is to make sure that while I add value to my audience through the different topics that I publish about to solve various problems for instance, I also add massive value to readers in ways that go beyond just one book. Subscribe to our newsletter to know when I publish new books, how I did market research, how I make money with the books and much, much more.

You can even ask questions on anything you want me to answer regarding publishing and everything else related to the topics of discussion.

Antony

Website: http://www.fantonpublishers.com/

Email: Support@fantonpublishers.com

Twitter: https://twitter.com/FantonPublisher

Facebook Page: https://www.facebook.com/Fantonpublisher/

My Ketogenic Diet Books Page: https://www.facebook.com/pg/Fast-Keto-Meals-336338180266944

Private Facebook Group For Readers: https://www.facebook.com/groups/FantonPublishers/

Pinterest: https://www.pinterest.com/fantonpublisher/

I look forward to hearing from you!

PSS: Let Me Also Help You Save Some Money!

If you are a heavy reader, have you considered subscribing to Kindle Unlimited? You can read this and millions of other books for just $9.99 a month)! You can check it out by searching for Kindle Unlimited on Amazon!

Printed in Great Britain
by Amazon